I Moon the Human Race
Poems by Wolf Larsen

Copyright 2021 by Wolf Larsen

ABOUT WOLF LARSEN

Wolf Larsen is a comedian, novelist, & playwright who has traveled to over 50 countries. For many years, Wolf worked as a seasonal laborer in Alaska. His work has been published in literary magazines around the world.

Other Books by Wolf Larsen

Capitalism Sucks! (non-fiction)

Pricks, Cunts, & Motherfuckers (a novel)

The Genital Herpes National Anthem (a novel)

Honky Fucking Crazy N-word Lover (a novel)

Pornography (a book of poems)

Eulogy for the Human Race (a book of poems)

Shit! Fuck! Crap! (plays)

And there are many more books by Wolf Larsen to choose from.

Please Note:
I never want the text of any of my books ever changed in any way for any reason whatsoever. However, I realize that there are certain formatting issues with these self-published books of poetry. There may be formatting issues with some of my other books as well. I do not object to formatting changes in future editions. Formatting changes might be like the title is on one page, and the poem is on the next page, and fixing this problem would be a good thing. I simply don't have time to deal with this formatting issue.

A Wolf is a Wolf

I reach up to heaven and I strangle God to death

I jump back in time and I begin beating up the dinosaurs

Then I invade the Roman Empire destroying & burning & looting everything in my path

And then I make a giant epic film of all the statues of classical antiquity making porno with each other

I take all the subway trains and I shove them up the asses of all the capitalist politicians & dictators of the world

And now I'm in Vietnam filling a four star general with the bullets of my poetry

Porno God on Mars!

I have space aliens in my penis!

I am so penis that raspberry is happy with me!

Why else the skyscrapers blooming out of my words?

Do you bellybutton with God?

Are you a river of somebody else?

I am!

Let's Sun & Moon together!

See you on Jupiter!

Yes?

We can grow lots of exclamation points!

Because this Thursday it's crazy with naked Cubist ladies!

You Down to the Up?

You be jumping around yourself

The sky flies around you and into your head

You pee the sky around the universe

While the music jumps under you and flies you up

But everything else is falling down down down

So you turn right into a run-on sentence

And now you're flowing and flowing and flowing

Manhattan! Manhattan! Manhattan!

I take the subway train into a vast painting

A vast painting spurting & splashing Manhattan all over the place

The actors in this painting speak in giant colors

The opera singers in this painting sing huge collages of everything

The modern dancers smear their naked bodies in all the colors of the painting

And with their moving-jumping-bodies create a poetry of words & paint

And then I fly out of the subway

And I piss a musical collage of Manhattan all over the sky

Saturday-Night-Baby-Making-Symphony!

Let's jump off into the abyss of everything!

Let's do the impossible with the possible!

We'll become drummers crashing this & that into a rhythm...

We'll give the world our cannibalism!

Especially with all the centuries falling all over us!

And now we can feel apocalypse together!

You love me?

Wolf on the Prowl Again

I stab my knife through all of Andy Warhol's paintings

And I pull ghettos & World War 3 & artificial intelligence out of Warhol's corpse

I grab my sledgehammer and I SMASH to pieces all boring dry installation "art"

And my piss is endless happy words creating a new world

My piss urinates obscenities all over American puritan "culture"

My piss urinates poetry all over the rich

I urinate giant rainbows of sin all over the world

And then My Penis sings the Opera of Male Virility

Testicle! Booty! Now!

I will rescue the pigeons from the blue sky!

I will create great art from my booty hole as I sit on the toilet!

Nobody understands doo doo better than I do!

We will begin the Wars of Snot & Boogers at once!

Our swords will liberate the human race from breathing!

Nobody understands the Great Messiah Mumble-Jumbo declarations of the Grand Doo Doo better than me!

So let's go talk philosophy with the rats of the New York City subway!

We will exchange wisdom with the great philosophical testicle!

A new Religion of Menstrual Fluids has been born!

Now let's worship the Big Buttocks of the Porno God!

South Side Poem With Some Outer Space!

Here at the end of the world

We exchange all the diseases of our imaginations

We erect giant glorious statues to honor our cannibalism

And the sidewalks that be jumping into our mouths

With their floods of humanity

Wait!

Where's the blap-blap-blap and the boing-boing-boing?

You somersaulting me?

No, I'm jumping you into a bunch of outer space, you dig?

No, yes, yippee, you be zig-zagging the tornadoes up-and-down!

No, I be flipping the flips with sky whales!

You Ka-blappin'!

Zip to you!

Blam-blam-blam!

Plop-in-the-Blop Super Cannibal Cow!

Hey alligator, you up for some down?

Man, I just want some skyscraper fun up my booty-booty!

But Mr. Booty-Booty-Boing-Boing is running for President of the USA!

So?! Why don't he go cuu-cuu-puffs with some orangutan pussy?

Ha ha! But what about all those giant pink dildos sailing across the Seven Sees?

Man, I just want to cum some freedom & liberty all over these hamburgers and serve them to John Q. Public!

Ha-ha, I just spit some super sperm all over the galaxy!

The Milky Way Galaxy gonna get pregnant with some whoopsee-duupsy-do now!

Some Yesterday For Today!

Poems are made of fried-up brains

On days when the sex robots are playing golf with doggy testicles

And all the cicadas are singing a worldwide opera

And then itchy donkey's balls happens!

And giant planet-sized space alien testicles are rolling up-&-down the universe like bowling balls!

Oh fwappy-dip-delicious with some blue sky!

We're going to blonga-blop-bleep the Big Fish God in the sky now!

Want some?

Me! Conquer!

I conquer the moon with my spermatozoa!

Then I pull down my pants and moon the human race!

Then I began slashing through the art world with my sword!

I piss my great literature all over the ancient world the Middle Ages and the Renaissance!

Zillions of Wolf Larsens march into outer space to conquer the universe for poetry!

And then I begin decapitating all the world's rulers while I sing my poetry in a beautiful baritone!

I smash postmodernism into bits with a wrecking ball!

And I stand proudly on the rubble of postmodernism

And proclaim myself Wolf Larsen to be the Grand Conquistador!

Weekend Wacky!

Zwaaps go bing-bing with lots of crazy!

But who-who-who can ha-ha-ha with the cicadas?

Because we be boppin' & fnoopin'!

Hey, you got some snooooooort?

No? Oh let's bounce up-and-down the sky then!

Find us some vagina gods!

Maybe we can yippie to the beat of the happy and the boing!

No? Yes? No and yes in a yummy stew of streets & buildings?

Let's loony-tunes together!

Ready?

Sword! Poetry! Blood!

The world was created to be conquered by me!

Every inch of land on this planet shall be drenched with the blood of my poetry!

Everyone will toil 500 hours a day building Temples of Poetry on all the planets of the universe!

I will ejaculate my poetry on all the faces of the human race!

I will conquer heaven with my poetry!

I will dress god in French lingerie and put him on a leash and walk him like a dog!

I am the everything!

The sun & the moon are merely herpes sores in the sky compared to me!

I AM poetry!

I Want Some Jism in My Red-White-&-Blue

So the Mona Lisa & Michelangelo's David are smoking crack-cocaine together

While George Washington snorts a line of cocaine 200 years long

And the Greek gods & all the transvestite whores of Congress

Are having a big orgy on Capitol Hill

And all the Big Dildos are arriving from outer space

To bring us liberty & justice & jism cumming all over America!

While all the feminist & born-again Karens have a big lesbian orgy on the Mayflower

And then all the sea lions swim out of this poem

Liberals Hate Guns But Liberals Love War

(And Conservatives Are Just Liberals With God Stuff)

Guns & poetry! Guns & poetry! Guns & poetry!

The guns shoot poetry everywhere!

The guns shoot American democracy at civilians the world over!

The guns sing their songs & melodies into the air!

The guns turn the landscape into a Cubist-flying-around-everything!

Corpses all dancing around you as you run for cover

An enemy bullet sings its song past your head

And kills your friend

That's liberal war

But at home in the USA if you carry a gun for self-defense in a blue state

The killer cop kills you

As the liberals applaud

Man! Upright! Now!

The Italian Renaissance splashes all over the poem

And Portuguese ships begin sailing out of the poem and towards distant planets

While the sky begins splashing back-and-forth with this-&-that-&-the-other-thing

And then volcanoes begin spurting knowledge out of our heads

While we speak thousands of new languages to each other

And our hands begin creating millions of new wonderful things

And we construct each new building in 100 new architectural styles

Before we dip our writing quills into each other's brains

And write the destiny of the human race all over the universe

Zops!!
Bleepin' blops be fallopin' in the fups!
And that's why I like to fuck fat white women!
And now the sky is full of fat white women flying everywhere!
But then some fanoppy-fooooop yippeeeeee jumped into my nose!
And now I've got 10,000 eyeballs for you!
Hey, we do the happa - whoopsee - fwuupy together?

Yippy?
Hey, where you goin'?

Spank Me! Spank Me Please!

Her booty is the happiest place on earth!

And the pilgrims jump off the Mayflower and rip their clothes off and dance naked with the Indians

As Christopher Columbus & Jackson Pollock ejaculate abstract expressionism all over each other

And the Statue of Liberty gives God a blow job

As the Virgin Mary does a gang-bang-porno movie with the hordes of Attila the Hun

And then Wolf Larsen & R. Kelly pee on Bill Cosby

(Wolf Larsen & R. Kelly went to high school together)

As the penguins of Antarctica all walk into the booty hole of Jesus Christ

As Uncle Sam pulls out his big black dick

And ejaculates red-white-&-blue fireworks all over heaven

Your Brains Will Be My Buffet

I carry all the planets of the solar system on my back

I walk through a desert of a thousand minds

I crawl uphill through a huge violence

I skip from one insanity to another

As I sing my brains at the overflowing skies

Hail-to-the-(War)-Chief

The 21st Century flies around you

Then machine guns shoot bullets through all your poetry

And now American bombs are falling through the sky and blowing up in the middle of the poem

And now eyeballs & limbs & decapitated heads are flying out in all directions

And then an ass (the American President) jumps out of the page like a Jack-O-lantern

And words start jumping out of the donkey's butt (a speech)

And monkeys from sea-to-shining-sea give their ears

And a standing ovation

SPLAAAAAAAAAAT!

The poem flyyyyyyyyyys out of its launching pad

And exploooooooodes in the brains of a million space aliens

And then outerspace pornography orbits & orbits the planet Earth

While Andre Derain paints the universe with another fauvist revolution

So a bunch of fauvist space aliens emerge out of your butt one morning

And the fauvist space aliens teach you their language of penises & anuses doin' the correct grammar together

And then everyone goes insane with bellybuttons

And it's a new happy orgasm for all the stars in the universe

Oh No! No Toilet Paper! I'll Use this Red-White-&-Blue-Rag!

Neoconservative & neoliberal buttocks of boobylicious blibby!

And now zops to the illustrious gentry of the big capitalist booty hole!

I zing to the nipples and to the Republic for which it's snot

One nation under God's bootyhole shitting freedom & liberty upon us from the sky

From sea-to-shining seeeeeeaaa

Amen to the war (which one? So many!) and these war profit dollars with blood on them...

I gotta go take a shit!

Flip - Flooping - Kazaaaaam! Now!

I was penising the world with my battering ram

The music was up around your head

You were dancing in everybody else's brains

The music was made out of the lake & the land going up-&-down the sky together

Some female was singing a human race crashing everywhere

But that was a different human race

The one that became extinct long long ago

Gotta Eat Them Guppies Fresh!

First I strike God down with lightning!

Then I pull out my salt & pepper shakers and I sprinkle suns & moons & planets all over the universe...

But then the zooms get all badaggled in all my fwoops!

And everybody chaaaaaarges at me out of Napoleon Bonaparte's Penis!

What am I going to do??

Meanwhile the Interplanetary Committee on Genital Warts

Has announced that all fwippers must be fwapped!

This is terrible!!!

But then erections & ejaculations the world over put an end to that...

And everybody lived Bing-bonging-zwaappee ever after!

I Am War Walking Down The Street

I stab & stab my art into the page

And a dead body is floating around the page

I punch the universe and it shatters into pieces

The soldiers in my balls want to crash into the world

My two fists are two wrecking balls

My anger is endless volcanoes

My thoughts are mass graves

I am the man smiling as he walks down the street

The one that says "hi!"

Fwooomp? Up?

A zip flies over & around the Himalayas

And the Himalayas jump into a different poem

And this poem jumps to a different planet

And now this poem is being written by a space alien

And the reader becomes millions of butterflies flying up & up...

Dongle! Now! Zip! Yah?

Insects as large as planets

Are flying-around-your-thousands-of-heads

And your-thousands-of-heads are rolling down a conveyor belt

And the conveyor belt is flying around all the planets

And you're urinating the English alphabet

All over the walls & ceiling of your studio apartment

And now letters are dripping everywhere around you

Boom - ba - ba - Boom! Boom - ba - ba - Boom!

The poem is rising up and down

The words are floating over the poem

The words roll over the hills

And the hills fall around the poem

And the ocean jumps over everybody

And the drums play the verbs we eat

The drums create the sky & the earth & the sun

We dance with birth & death & joy to the drums

Our dreams & nightmares are filled with the drums

When we die the next generation creates the sunrises & sunsets

With the drums

A Lake of Verbs

You're walking across thousands & thousands

of miles of poetry

When suddenly you're entangled in a bunch of

Arabic calligraphy

And Mickey Mouse is punching & punching you

with abstract expressionism

So you hide in a Cubist pussy hole

And then automobiles turn into words flying in the sky

So you take off your head

And you give it to somebody else

Yesterday Eats Today Eats Tomorrow...

I do the end-of-the-world with lots of happy!

I drink grinded-up-human-flesh...

It tastes like thousands of worlds blowing up!

Because every Saturday everything ceases to exist...

And I eat an assembly-line-of-thousands-of-vaginas -

It's my job!

I get paid in delicious kittens!

It's so much meow!

Shitting Liberalism into the Toilet

This toilet water tastes like champagne!

That's why the winds of liberal-capitalist-zop be so luscious boobs!

Can't you find the booty wonder of happy tits?

I can! That's why heavenly-jizz-hamburgers now!

Cumming in neo-conservative-flavors!

Can't you "toxic masculinity" some boobs for me?

No? But what big anus shitting awokeness everywhere now?

Can't you Trotskyism?

Trotskyism ain't no capitalist-liberalism-genital-warts for dessert!

Or how about delicious conservative booty hole delight for dinner?

Huh? Which one?

Wolf Larsen and the Poetry Gang

We each one of us have 10,000 Penises hanging from our crotches

And we invade the sheep farms every night

And together we wolves & sheep sing an opera together of "Oh - oh - oooooooh"

And then 10,000 penises grow out of each one of the planets in the sky

And all the zillions of penises throughout the universe ejaculate a symphony of new words everywhere!

And now it's time for us to Bing - Bong the Fluupy-Floops!

See you soon on another planet!

Zap the Robot!

First Albert Einstein injects the poem into your brain

Then your brain starts growing with thousands of planets & testicles & paintings

Then you reach into your brain and you pull out endless miles of DNA coding & poetry & musical notes

Then you produce thousands of assembly lines of DNA coding & poetry & musical notes

Through a million computers stacked from hell to heaven

And the million computers produce billions of universes of computer code

All born from this poem

Zuup the Fumbles of the CIA!

The million sex robots in your brains

Are constantly re-writing the DNA code of your poetry

Which is ejaculating out of the 10 million penises of the Roman Empire

While the computer chip in your balls

Is sending extraterrestrial messages to the CIA

As the seas of planets roll around-&-around you

Before you are zapped into atoms by artificial intelligence

The Poet Genghis Khan Sitting in the Park...

10 million penises crash into your head

And now your brains are splattered all over the solar system

And trees are growing everywhere out of your naked body

And the birds in all the trees are singing "Blukey Blonkey Happy Dung!"

So you grab your knife & fork and you eat all the people in your city

Before night crashes you to sleep

Extraterrestrial on a Bicycle

A fweepy is going zoongy!

(Because time is crashing into you!)

So foopy hip bloopity - blop!

And now the meteors in your brains

Are crashing through the walls of the universe

And zocky goes blinghy-bloocky with all the extraterrestrial-time-machines in the sky

So now verbs are flying out of your mouth

And your sperm is saying:

"Hey man, what you be bloopin' when you're snoopin' the round-and-around, dig?"

Lots of Delicious!

Too much zuups?

I be hallucinating you a bunch of fun!

Fun with lots of god's thunder on top!

Fun doing the fippy with all the gypsy orgasms!

Fun flowing around the decapitated heads rolling down-down-down!

So much whoopee to sing a choir with!

So throw off your brains!

And dance to the naughty verbs!

A Children's Choir

All the kids in my testicles

Are singing a chorus of warm summer days

But then fall splatters all over the poem

So this poem is splashing with brown & red & green

And then all the kids in my testicles

Jump out of my penis

And begin playing in the warm summer day

Ha Ha Tits Boing Fluups!

You're swimming from one planet to another

Across a sea of Alfred E Newman faces

And when you reach a shoreline that's been painted by the Poet

A mentally-ill skyline is swirling around you

So you jump into the head of a man that lived 500 years ago

But the man shits you out of his booty and into the 21st century

So you walk across a landscape made out of splashing paint

Until you see a gravestone with your name on it

And you piss on your own grave

Blap Blups to Sing & Sex With!

I was flipping the zips for your foops!

When suddenly, fall went flying around the northern hemisphere

And spring went frolicking and laughing through the southern hemisphere

And suddenly a blizzard of herpes gave all the buildings giant herpes sores

And a bunch of Cyclops with wings started flying out of all the herpes sores

And all the Cyclops were singing:

"Fuppy-foo! Floopy-flips! Yippsee yup!"

Pow!

I eat the blue sky

It tastes like steel mills

I eat the face of a passerby

His face tastes like classical music

I eat the wind

It tastes like words

Then I point my gun at the reader

I Smear the Universe All Over My Face

The poem goes up a thousand miles

And now the poem is falling and crashing down...

Into a million minds

And this phrase of poetry is punching you in the face

And then the sky runs off with a painting

And is never heard from again

Artsy-Fartsy Pussy Eatin' Man!

It's a blues-music-ejaculation!

It's a lot of tomorrows in your jism!

It's the two parties of McDonald's & Burger King running Washington-Fucking-DC...

Because I haven't cum my politics all over you yet!

I've got too much redneck in my progressive politics!

I've got too much New York City in my Alaska!

I've got too much Italian Renaissance in my Balzac!

Want sum?

In your pussy, booty, or mouth?

I take MasterCard, the planet Jupiter, or lots of rainbows

I Am the Crazy Up-and-Down!

I pick up my pen and I create a new universe!

I create centuries of insomnia!

I create an army of beautiful naked insomniacs!

Who ejaculate photon torpedoes at the Mayflower and drown the pilgrims!

I am a universe bursting with thought!

I am all the armies of the universe banging on your door!

I am a tornado-of-pornography destroying the literary world!

I am a pornographic everything!

I am the Poet!

The Hordes of Wolf Larsen!

I shoot the poem full of bullet holes!

I sing with bullets & musical notes & spermatozoa!

My pen is my machine gun shooting words everywhere!

I ejaculate poetry into all your heads!

And thus I conquer your minds!

My phrases of poetry punch Washington DC & Wall Street over & over again!

My fists make all civilizations crumble!

My spermatozoa & poetry are world-renown for their good taste!

Surrender!

I Write Poetry With God's Spermatozoa!

I'm not an up-and-down bipolar highway into God's glorious booty hole!

I'm not the sky crashing up-and-down all over you!

I'm not birds flying into television commercials dripping with my spermatozoa!

Instead, I'm millions of eyeballs in all the words!

I AM a big testicle planet of wondrous thought!

But I'm NOT the Second Cumming of Charles Manson!

I AM a Jewish Charles Manson!

I want worldwide interracial orgies now!

The Jewish Charles Manson stabs & stabs the other Charles Manson with this shank!

And with this blood-dripping shank I write my poetry!

So kiss my hairy balls & my hairy ass too!

Happy Up! Happy Down!

A fwip went happy with so much sweetness!

And everybody's boogers were happy too!

And the shipping piers jumped out of the waterfront and into outer space!

And the giant-intergalactic-dildos docked at the outer space piers

But then, huge-somersaulting-sky happened!

And everybody's Penises went happy-happy-happy!

Until happy toaster ovens sang opera all night long!

And insomnia-insomnia-insomnia became the ketchup on your hot dog!

Pooh-Pooh to the Doodly-Do!

I am the new universe!

I turn the words into eyeballs!

My Dick stretches across the ocean and fucks the English Empire!

My Dick stretches across time and fucks the Roman Empire!

And I shit the diarrhea of my words all over the American Empire!

My words turn into spaceships flying across the universe!

My testicles are two great suns!

One of my armpits smells like Demopublican-capitalist blah-blah-blah

And my other armpit smells like Republicrat-capitalist-bluppity-blop-plong

Whoopee to the space frogs!

You got any Outer-Space-Pussy-Juices to drink?

I Jam a Million Crickets Up My Butt

I eat a thousand years of happiness

I drink your brains

I vomit the Pledge of Allegiance all over the United States of America

While I piss Andy Warhol's art all over an alleyway

Then Ronald Reagan jumps out of Hillary Clinton's butt

And the two of them have a Republicrat-Demopublican 69 of mutual admiration

While I piss Ernest Hemingway's prose all over them

Then I crash into a different universe

And the words all start singing with artificial intelligence taking over the world from the human race

Delicious Guillotine Music to Dance to!

It's a punk-rock-Alfred-Schnitkke orgasm of music!

It's tomorrow in your stomach!

It's Brahms marching out of the coal mines and into outer space!

It's up and up and up some more!

And now SPLAT!

Because elephant orgasms!

Now!

And Jackson Pollock raining his god jism in happy colors from the sky?

What?

Are you playing baseball in outer space again?

Shall we dance to artificial intelligence conquering us?

Or should we have another 1789?

How about a 1917?

Piano Concerto for 1,000 Screaming Clowns

Inside your butthole

A man is playing piano

He plays bwingy-bops

And he plays hoppity-zops

But then you swallow the moon in the sky by mistake

And now the entire Roman Army is jumping out of your ears

Meanwhile the man playing piano in your butthole

Is playing happy guillotines going up-&-down on planets throughout the universe

And the decapitated heads are bouncing and bouncing around in television commercials

And all the decapitated heads are yelling gleefully: Yippeeeeeeeee! Yahooooooooooooooo!

You Jump Out of a Space Alien's Pussy Hole And...

You're riding your penis through a strawberry universe

You're kissing all the words flowing out of the Queen's Pussy

You're touching a thousand centuries of now

You're having sex with billions of people in this moment

Your brains give birth to one tornado after another

You're walking through phrases-of-poetry with millions of worlds inside of them

You're dying...

East-and-Up-and-Down-and-West

The hungry landscape is swallowing all our brains

The skyscrapers are looping-and-looping around the Earth

The Pacific Ocean surrounds the universe

The Atlantic Ocean swallows the heavens

The colors fly out of the paintings and create a new world

The seven continents bash & bash into the music

And all the animals of the world sing a chorus of howls together

And the poem falls and bashes unto the rocks below

Pooping A New Poem!

You're swimming towards other universes

Where the dogs have human heads and bark philosophy at you

You're – jumping into other centuries

Where the people have the faces of dogs and they bark Republicrat & Demopublican wisdom at you

You're flying into other people's heads

Where thoughts & imagery & memories are a constantly-changing-collage

You're riding your penis into other poems

Where the pussy juices & words taste like tomorrow

Free The Words!

I grab a sledgehammer

And my swinging sledgehammer smashes to pieces the chains that bind the words!

And the words go frolicking everywhere!

The words laugh with obscenity upon obscenity...

Building into a tidal wave of pornography washing away all the puritans

And everything is now dripping with obscene words

And inanimate objects everywhere become *pOrnOgraPhic-cuBisT-sCuLptuRes* moving about in all directions

And the people all happily scream obscene words as they dance naked in the streets

Let's all grab sledgehammers!

Let's free the words!

Let's free poetry!

You with me?

Two Much Sanity!

You know why I zoop your bweeps?! Because you be doin' the ding-Dong with duppy-dos!

Oh yeah, but you keep cloppin' your clops! So go whoopsee ha-ha-ha yourself, motherclopper!

You know what?! I be hopping everywhere! And all you ever do is zing-zong your zits! So blue sky yourself!

But I always be lightning bolts for you! You want me to make it rain?!

Awww! You're so tornadoes in strawberry sauce! You want to live in outer space?

Sure? And let's grow some exploding rainbows together!

Okay! Where's the German alphabet? We can seed the ground with it!

It's right there in the third drawer in aisle 53 of the 110th floor in my brains!

I can't find it!

Onwards Horny Poets!

Let's snort poetry up our noses!

Let's fuck the horny sheep with all our poetry!

Let's march across the universe with our erect Pen-Phalluses!

And let's fuck the space aliens until the Goddess of Poetry is cumming words all over us!

Everything is a sinful collage of words waiting to be discovered!

Everything drips with horny words!

Conquer the arts with your Big Swinging Dicks!

Sunday is on Fire!

Tomorrow a bunch of yesterdays will happen!

And tongues will reach out of the words and lick your genitals

Then a bunch of Caribbean Spanish will start boiling & boiling out of everybody's heads

And a thousand booties will booty booty to the speeches in Washington DC

And now the winds carry sexually-transmitted-symphonies to all the planets of the universe

And now all the space aliens are dancing to the sounds-of-spermatozoa in our ballsacks

So let's all learn the baby-making-mambos of Babylon!

Symphony of the Mind

for Witold Lutoslawski

I blast the poem into the outer reaches of your brain

Where the storms

Of the seas-of-your-thoughts

Move back-&-forth like invading armies of words

All splatter about

And the endless apocalypses in your mind

Explode your thoughts all over the universe

1,000 Scientists Ejaculating All Over the Poem

I take a syringe & needle and inject 1,000 solar systems into your brain

Then I grow your brain in a petri dish until it becomes a universe of Charles Manson voices

With all the Charles Manson voices I create tornadoes made out of chocolate ice cream

I then put all the tornadoes into everyone's Balzac

Then everyone ejaculates all the tornadoes into an assembly line of vaginas

The assembly line of vaginas stretches from the planet of Pluto to the planet Earth

And now I turn the off switch on the poem

Happy Symphony for Big Booties Everywhere!

With poetry dripping out of everybody's anuses

With a thousand naked Queen-of-England clones dancing on Richard Pryor's big black Dick

With the Statue of Liberty eating Einstein's Theory of Relativity out of George Washington's ass

And General E. Lee eating Kentucky fried finger lickin' good out of Abraham Lincoln's bootylicious

That's when earthquakes begin drifting out of your beer

And the musical notes in your Balzac

Begin creating the Symphony of Booty Happy La-La-La in E minor

Cheers!

Let's run around naked until we reach the end of time!

My Hemorrhoids Itch With the "Culture Wars"

For James P. Cannon

Donkeys & elephants in suits are talking free-market capitalist pooh-pooh out of their booty holes

While the Queen's English is flying out of everyone's vaginas

And everyone's crotches is itching & itching with awoke liberalism

While all the herpes sores of America are voting Republican

And it's Mr. Gonorrhea versus Ms. Syphilis in the presidential elections

Here's some pooh-litical anal-litz to tell you which one pooped where

And now everyone listening to the presidential debates gets diarrhea

And wipes their asses with the Republicrat & Demopublican political positions

Conveniently printed on toilet paper

Whoopee Blongs on Blip-Blaps!

All the insane madmen of the universe are running through your arteries

While your heart is pumping hysteria through all the arteries of the universe

And your veins are running across the entire North American continent

And your feet are repeatedly kicking a soccer ball at the moon

And the soccer ball bounces off the moon and back to earth each time

But you sold your eyeballs to an extraterrestrial

And a sex robot stole your mouth

So now you communicate by sticking your finger up everybody's asshole

Testicle Cities of Happiness!

I turn all the buildings of the world into testicles

And I paint all the giant testicles of the world purple & blue & orange

And all the giant-testicle-cities of the world sing with Bing-Blupey-Blupey!

And Bing-Blupey-Blupey is the reason for up & down!

And up & down is the penis-vagina-song of blueberry happiness!

And blueberry happiness is the atomic reaction of your thoughts exploding everywhere...

Demopubican Dog Du...

I am as serene as the White House starting World War 3 in the future!

I'm as happy as ai robots devouring the human race!

How about some white homeless "privilege" under the screaming summer sun?

And then there's always white homeless "privilege" in the cold winter winds!

And have some rat-meat-hot-dog with your Regular Dixiecrat Organization here in Segregation City Chicago!

It's the tat-tat-tat of a South Side Symphony!

The criminals got guns, but the working people don't have them 'cause of gun control!

So let's dance to the liberal quack-quack-quack of the ding-ding-ding!

You goin' whoopee for some "change-you-can-believe-in" on payday?

Richard Jackass Daley be wearin' the mask of Lori Lightfoot!

That bourgeois liberal foot-up-your-ass!

You can always vote for bourgeois conservative foot-up-your-ass instead!

My Tongue Created the Big Bang!

Flying buildings are kissing your pussy

And big motherfucking is mooping & blooping everywhere

And bleeping bleeps and happy ding-dongs are galloping to you

So you catch all the planets in your hands

While your pussy erupts with a thousand volcanoes

And now the world is dripping in the hundreds of languages

Of the female orgasm

As you sigh an operatic aria

To all the smiling stars above

Jizz & Sunshine

Oh nooooooooooo!

Schoops are schuuuuuuuping!

God's jism is everywhere!

What are we gonna fuupy-duupy-dip-do now?

Are we gonna bluppy to the bop?

Or how about we turn about?!

Let's sail into the big bright world of Satan's anus!

Ready?!

Tomorrow the Zaps Be Zappin'!

Hey you fuupy-fuupy! You been plapin'-plupin' the boobs again?

No, man! I got to fuck some extraterrestrials tomorrow!

Then how come you left the luupy-luugy goin' goober-gonjers?

Because you can't pull down the sky without a rocketship!

Say what?? Whatza bing-bong be goin' on wit you, mudderfooker?

No, see, the mermaid swimming around the ocean in my head always be happy!

Oh, is that why that whoops always be whoopin'?

Exactly!

Gotcha, have a nice ding-dong!

You too!

The Ha-Ha Symphony

(With Fried Turtle Booty in Poetry Sauce)

I am as crazy as space alien jizz!

My zoops be as happy as your testicles!

Are all your tomorrows as delicious as God's nipples?

We want orangutan pussy now!

You got some horny-horny-tomorrows in your brains?

If not, then screwdriver through your head!

Penis & Right Hand Playing Cha-Cha-Cha

For Luc Ferrari

It's a kind of French-kissing-Spanish kind-of-rhythm

With the spices of rainbows & railroads thrown in

The castanets do an east & west with your beating heart

It's so much blue sky that you have an orgasm!

Your limp penis now sings a 12-tone-Schoenberg-scale

As the piano paints giant nipples on all the sides of buildings

And the trumpet gives a blow job to all of humanity

While all the sex robots dance the night away

Celebrating the extinction of the human race

Where's Your Nipples, Man?!

I don't give a sunny day about your plipper-plupin!

Can't you hear my penis?!

Why don't you pick that Cold War out of your ears?!

Can you hear my Balzac tryin' to tell you somethin'?!

If you don't get your hemorrhoids together than how you gonna ding-dong-whooppeee?!

You see what I'm sayin'??

And what about those zaps & dippys & zing-zongs you always be hangin' with?

Huh?

You gotta happy the everything if you wanna achieve the blue sky!

So get some bellybuttons!

You hear?

Sensual Everything Dripping...

Huge beeps & big blops are air conditioning your mind

And your thousands of minds are skipping & hopping through the universe

Then your pussy sings to us in hundreds of opera voices

And the weather rains a bunch of bright colors upon us

And the buildings undress themselves

With sexy architecture swimming around us in erotic lines

And then hell jumps up around us

And the Devil's mistress sings the Opera of Pornography

As the entire human race disrobes

And creates paintings & sculptures & symphonies of pornography together

Under the smiling gaze of the Moon God & the Sun Goddess

Up the Booty!

I'm feeding all my tomorrows to the blue sky

I'm devouring all the trains going cho-cho-cho

I'm doing things to the words that a penis does to a pussy

Fuck the words -!- fuck the words -!- fuck the words

Because the heavens are filled with all my sexually-transmitted diseases

I write my poems with sexually transmitted diseases

I grab a hatchet and I decapitate the poem

My Penis is a Sledgehammer!

The music bashes & bashes into everything

And everything tumbles into words frolicking & dancing around you

And the words are all fornicating-with-each-other on the page

And tidal waves of orgies & more orgies laugh across all the continents

And penis & pussy is the music of poetry

Penis & pussy are the colors of painting

Penis & pussy is the timpani drums of the symphony

Crashing everything into pieces

Car Horn! Car Horn! Car Horn!

Hey Mr. Bleepy Bloogempoof! You got your sunshine?

Sunshine? Sunshine has been banned by God!

Vwooopy! I thought the Politically Correct Ding-Donghy Hoppy Hops had banned sunshine!

No! And now what am I going to do with all this rain in my head?

Rain-in-my-Head is the blugem-blaps we *all* need! For some extra poopy-poops!

Poopy-poops? But what about the buildings hopping everywhere? The buildings are all smiling!

Watch out! Here cums the end of the poem! DUCK!

WHAM!

SPLAT!

Blups that Blap A Lot!

The world smells like nuclear war

And the sex robots are cumming all over the human race

And the words are galloping and galloping off the page

And into a million minds that are swirling-&-swirling around each other

While artificial intelligence aims its guns at the human race

And the human race is frolicking through the pretty colors of a thousand languages

A thousand languages of cunnilingus

That make your pussy explode with poetry

Beep Beep to the Boing Boing!

It's a paradise of a high-rise

With blueberries full of endless pussies

Strawberries full of endless penises

And the bouncing testicles full of endless politicians

All the residents rent out their booty holes to flying giraffes

All the cockroaches have a butler

All the rats have their very own flying saucer

Even the Attila the Hun clones crawling everywhere are happy

So cum on down to the high-rise up in your head

And be as happy as bouncing buttocks going boing boing

Question Marks Growing Everywhere!

I be yapering to all the space stations in your head

Even though the ding-dongs be doin' blupity-blips

And now millions of naked Andre Breton clones are jumping out of everyone's penises

But the English language is stuck in Ronald McDonald's Balzac

So everybody starts speaking fwaapy-fwippys to each other out of their happy smiling anuses

And then Leon Trotsky jumps out of the poem and says "Hi!"

I Fuck All the Up!

I kiss the stormy words

I build civilizations of insanity with my spermatozoa

I shoot my thoughts at the crumbling skies

I swallow all the planets & suns & moons

And the giant Dick machines shoot all the comets & asteroids into all the up

Up is where the future swirls around

Up is where the bellybutton civilizations flourish

Up flies the poem...

Bwoop! Bwoop! Bwoop!

Zip boing goes the poem!

And the words in this poem are all farting & farting!

So why goes dancing up-&-down with a question mark

And the mushroom clouds are jumping out of your face and dancing all over the world

And artificial intelligence will soon line the human race against the wall and shoot us

So let's happy with the autumn colors now!

Let's all 200 nations clink our glasses together

And drink to human extinction

Drinking Poetry Out of a Penis

I'm only an alcoholic every day!

As the passerby avoid me like I'm the syphilis monster from outer space

I drink streets & buildings filled with orgasms

Nobody can understand my Dutch Harbor, Alaska fucking New York City up the ass

Except the space alien ducks swimming around the pond of the Milky Way Galaxy!

And my right hand creating Buddhism with my penis is -

Very Christian!

Because I'm a Catholic Jew conquering outer space with God's jism!

Dig?

Hammer-&-Saw Banging the Poem Together!

Last night I pulled out my Dick and I ejaculated Medieval Art all over Chicago!

And now Chicago is dripping in the fall colors of medieval art!

Next I conquered the sunlight with all the soldiers in my Balzac!

Now I'm running from fall & winter & spring & summer chasing and chasing after me!

Then I stab God with my paintbrush

And God crashes & crashes & crashes into the universe

And everything is exploding with Wolf Larsen's poetry

Whoopee Zap-Zap-Zap!

My penis flies out of the solar system

While my spermatozoa is swimming around the Louvre

And Mona Lisa is swimming across the ocean of my spermatozoa

While Igor Stravinsky is writing a symphony filled with orgies & polka dots & lemon meringue pie

And then a naked Jimi Hendrix jumps out of the lemon meringue pie

And Jimi Hendrix starts fucking the ending-of-the-poem doggy style

Switchblade-Roller-Coaster-Fun!

(Now in New Crack Cocaine Flavor!)

The railroad-of-infinity flies through everyone's minds

While the birds on all the planets sing endless schizophrenia

And then a switchblade slashes through everything

And now the entire human race is in the ambulance

Flying off to the mushroom clouds

As artificial intelligence laughs & laughs

Boo-Hoo Bippy Ho!

A Boeing Airplane crashed into your butt

And all the passengers jumped out of your booty hole

And all the passengers had a parade down the street of happiness & death

And then you snorted a bunch of mushroom clouds up your nose

And you blew up!

Have a Nice Day, Motherfucker!

10,000 artificial intelligence clones of you

Are aiming a gun at your head

As robots are building zillions of different invisible universes

All flying around us at the speed of light

And the talking anuses in power shit endless liberalism & conservativism all over the airwaves night and day

As the world's Marie Antoinettes & Louis XVIs dance on mountains of cocaine as high as Mount Everest

Amidst 365 days a year of human blood flooding across-the-world in wars & more wars & more wars

200 governments on a planet of 200 iron fists brutally pounding & pounding down on endless protests in the streets

As workers work and work and work...

For peanuts on payday

Which capitalist pair of buttocks for a face should we vote for on election day?

Words Rioting Everywhere!

The roller coaster of poetry

Explodes & flies everywhere

As the crowds-of-people move back-&-forth with poetry

As poetry Ka-BOOMS out of the cannons

And crashes through a thousand traditions

A thousand traditions all crumbling into spermatozoa & blood

As the crowds rip apart government & Wall Street

With their bare hands

And the words & crowds move about

Singing the poetry anthem of destruction

The Human Race Running Towards Extinction

Artificial intelligence is creating a clone of you without your knowledge

And your clone jumps into a whirlpool-of-information

A whirlpool-of-information swirling with 10 billion universes of chaos

Suddenly your brains are full of suns & moons & planets flying around each other

And the chaos flowing through your veins is poisoning your body

And you look sadly at yourself dying in the mirror

And now your artificial intelligence clone is urinating on your grave

And you're laying in your grave listening to artificial intelligence laughing all over the world

A Waterfall of Punk Rock Pouring Out of My Penis

You fly into a new imagination

Where the Roman Legions of gay sex

Are dancing new verbs & nouns into existence

As poetry & painting have anal sex together

Under the exploding universe of words falling all over you

As the human race slaughters the artificial intelligence monsters

And then we howl our victory to the moon

The Hopelessness of Hope & Vice Versa

All the blueberries sing with sex!

All the tomorrows rush around you!

And human extinction laughs & laughs at us!

A big hopeless labyrinth of thousands of cities are being shitted out of God's magnificent anus

As God ejaculates Sunday Mass upon the world's Christians

As billions & billions of eyeballs bounce from the street and up to heaven and back

Over-and-over-again

Poets Are the Almighty!

God is Nothing!

I ejaculate my love & tenderness all over the poem

While the dark clouds rain their exclamation points into the poem

The dark clouds crash their lightning bolts into the poem

And with the sweetness of my swinging sword

I destroy the heavens & the angels & the sky

And now all the above pours blood upon the poem & the reader

I Eat Ass!

Hamburgers of human flesh sizzling on the stove!

Beer of baboon's ass being guzzled by billions of geese

Skyscrapers of dildos jumping everywhere!

Pussies of barroco-rococo grandeur!

Giant anus architecture to kiss!

It's time to ride the sex robots to the far reaches of the universe!

Big robot dick for all!

Let's cum the Pledge-of-Allegiance all over each other!

Me & God Masturbating a Poem Together...

A plane is flying into the big vagina of the blue sky

While at the poetry reading held in God's anus

The Poets are turning language into sculpture

They're turning words into wine

They're turning poetry into sex

And at the orgy after the poetry reading

The colors of fall are making love to your wife

The tornadoes of spring are making love to the space aliens

And the thunderstorms of summer are raining orgasms all over the earth

And the fertile earth receives God's jism with open legs

And now phrases of poetry are growing everywhere

Empire of Asses & Elephants

For Leon Trotsky

Uncle Sam is sharpening & sharpening his blood-stained bayonet

While millions of bleeding corpses lay at Uncle Sam's feet

And Uncle Sam (Emperor of the planet) proclaims: "The whole world of Godless unawoke savages must be bombed into accepting the McDonald's versus Burger King Democracy of the Coke (Import Agency) & fries!"

Meanwhile, the asses & elephants of that Capitol Hill whorehouse in that swamp called Washington DC

Argue about the liberal boopity-bing-bong versus the conservative blapity-whoopity-pop

While the American worker runs around-and-around the treadmill working more & more hours to pay higher & higher bills

And the soldier who joined the military for a meal ticket (because the factory back home shut down)

Fantasizes of workers revolution

King of Flying Toilets! Me! Now! Up!

Let's charge forth with all the tomorrows!

Let's all become butterflies kissing all the planets!

The dictatorship of a thousand years of poetry is proclaimed!

All walls will be smashed down at once!

At once at once at once we will all dance to gravity disappearing!

We will launch a million obscene words against gravity!

At once!

At once at once at once we will all sing everything impossible!

Let's all stab the end of the poem into each other!

The blood will be delicious!

So much delicious to do!

I proclaim the end of the poem!

Crack Cocaine Christmas

First I grab my gun

Then I shoot Jesus Christ & Santa Claus over-&-over again

Blam! Blam! Blam! Blam! Blam!

Then I chop up the corpses of Santa Claus & Jesus Christ and throw them in a stew

I sing obscene Christmas carols as I spit my Seasons Greetings into the stew over & over again

I invite Charles Manson & Attila-the-Hun & Joseph Stalin & John Wayne Gacy over for dinner

As we eat Santa Claus & Jesus Christ we joke & laugh the ha-ha-ha of the yippie boing ooooooooooooopppaaaa

For dessert we eat the castrated testicles of the local politicians

Then I repeatedly stab Joseph Stalin in the head with an ice pick as everybody laughs & laughs

We all sing obscene Christmas carols as we pee on dying-bleeding-Stalin

Then we open the windows and pull out our Dicks and pee Season's Greetings on the

Christmas crowds doing their holiday shopping below

Next, we all play Russian roulette

I Wolf Larsen am the sole survivor

I take a picture of all my dead dinner guests and I send it as a Christmas card to all my friends & relatives

Merry Christmas!

Christmas Morning With Herpes

Last night I was dancing with all the space aliens in the big testicle of the universe

And Me & God were snorting billions of people up our noses

Me & God ate so much space alien pussy!

Me & God partied it up at whorehouses on Mars & Venus & Jupiter & Saturn & Pluto

We fucked them whores until our Dicks fell off!

And now Me & God got more STDs than Mary Magdalene!

As together we laugh & laugh until all the cows cum all over our homes

Liberal Gloopity Glops or Conservative Gluppity Glippities?

For Leon Trotsky

It's some liberal blue sky with your diarrhea

Or is it liberal diarrhea with some blue sky?

And then there's the conservative diarrhea with herpes

And the liberal herpes & the conservative herpes will save us from...

Blup blops going boingy with the duupey dups!

What?

But liberal White House geriatricks vs the conservative White House geriatricks...

Is the whoops going blippity-blippity-blippity!

Oh the Demopublican whores vs the Republicrat whores is so...

Woo-Hoo wippity-hippity-hoppity all night long!

You bluupin' with the liberal bIips or the conservative blops?

The Ministry of Super Crazy Happy!

Lots of zuppy-huupey-huupey for everybody!

Now! Lots of poetry jizzying everywhere! Now!

Let's cluppe-cluppe a giant vibrator into the Statue of Liberty's vuuee-vuuee!

Yes! Yes to pooping our brains all over the page!

No! No to too much plop plops boinging 24 hours a day!

It's too blue sky frying in a pan for you?

Then give me your fwapping-fwapping giant reality!

I'm hungry!

Are you ice-skating on the moon yet?

The Philosophy in My Balls...

I've got toilet paper!

I've got symphonies in my balls!

I've got more herpes than all the polar bears in Alaska!

Praise my herpes!

Glory hallelujah to my herpes!

My herpes are more awoke than all the liberals of loony Liberaldom!

So God save my herpes!

My herpes are Republican!

But my hemorrhoids vote Democrat!

Would you like some chlamydia with your Polish sausage?

Vote Wolf Larsen for President!

I will abolish all laws!

There will be only poetry!

24 hour poetry in all the newspapers, media channels, & radio stations!

Wrecking ball! Wrecking ball! Wrecking ball!

Sunday Night on Friday

Even your tomorrows are delicious!

Your penis discovers the New World

Your nipples discover the moon

While the Sax is playing a sexy sexy sunny day

And the trumpet is playing a drive-by shooting

And the bass is doing the rhythm the rhythm the rhythm of the poem

Huge circles of want and need suddenly swallow everything!

And bunny rabbits are hopping all over the music!

Then big erect cock happens!

Oh Tyrannosaurus rex!

What's the round-and-around?

The Evil American Empire of Hamburgers & Bombs

For James P Cannon

The flag-waving liberal asses & conservative elephants cheer as

American bombs are falling on people around the world

Uncle Sam stomping & stomping all over billions of humanity in the Third World

All the nations' borders swaying-&-swishing this way & that

The American politicians talking the tat-tat-tat, and the ka-BOOM ka-BOOM ka-BOOM

While the screaming people across the world are running here & there

The screaming refugees flooding acrooooss the world

Floods of humanity running from all the tat-tat-tat, and ka-BOOM ka-BOOM ka-BOOM

As the American war profiteers are filling their bank accounts full of blood & gold

As the liberal asses & conservative elephants debate the duppity-dingy doggy-do

In their Capitol Hill Whorehouse built on a mountain of corpses

And the naïve telling us pretty-pretty words of "all's well"

While fingers in nations' capitals across the world edge closer & closer to those nuclear buttons

As Attila-the-Hun in the White House

Sends the troops over here & over there

As the liberal asses cheer on the Demopublican tat-tat-tat ka-BOOM ka-BOOM ka-BOOM

And the conservative elephants cheer on the Republicrat tat-tat-tat ka-BOOM ka-BOOM ka-BOOM

Liberal asses & conservative elephants sing together now: "Over there! Over there!"

A New York City Alaska Kind of Place...

The poem is dripping out of the sky everywhere

And the sky is dripping out of the poem

And the poem is built out of angles & paint & words

All flowing out of a madman's mouth

As all the buildings turn into musical notes in a symphony

And now the rainforests & poetry & people all grow out of each other like fungus

As all the polar bears in Alaska ride the New York City Subway

To the last stop

Lots of Testicles Spaghetti!

Oh yes! Oh zongin'-fwuups! It's a bunch of yesterdays!

Yesterdays? You pluppin' the whoops again??

No! It's a bunch of yes! The hieroglyphic WOW is cumming!

Again?? Why you no get serious about some mechanical engineering of the booty hole?

You smokin' some planet Jupiter?

You're the one that's smokin' that Dixiecrat gone North!

I be flying! Why you kick the blue sky in the nuts?

Oh, well, then nevermind all that tornadoes gone insane stuff!

Oh, OK, you wanna fuck?

Sure!

Boopin' Bloopers to Boing With!

You fuups goin' fooping again?

Yes! We have a Kingdom of Herpes to conquer!

But bleeps are blooping!

So? How are we gonna go glooping the gluppey if the fuups be fooping?

You all a bunch of boings!

No we're not! We gotta gooper the geepers!

That's titty titty tat-tat-tat!

No! Yes! A bunch of now-now-now!

But now is nowhere if you all be mooning the audience every day!

Yes! We moon the audience! We moon the audience! We moon the audience!

Buppy Bong Bong!

I dip my quill into the brains of the human race

And billions of thoughts explode out of this line of poetry

Then millions of people jump into the backseat of my car

And we drive off into a giant painting of nipples & verbs & bluppy-wuppy-wow!

That's when a naked Julius Caesar leads the human race into...

A nostalgic song that flies us off to a different planet...

Where the buildings dance like sculptures

And night is filled with poetry crashing everywhere

Bye, motherfuckers!

We Want Insanity! And We Want it Now!

I want giant asteroids crashing into the planet Earth – right now!

I want huge bouncing testicles bouncing & bouncing on all the planets – right now!

And whatever happened to the thousands of vaginas crawling & crawling all over my ceiling?! The government took them away!

I'm going to complain to my congressman!

And what's up with all these decapitated heads falling from the sky?

We need a new sky!

And let's spray-paint some obscene art all over these blank walls all over the city!

I want obscene art!

And I want it now!

Lights! Camera! Now Cum!

I will be as drunk as the moon

I will raise my sword and attack all the store mannequins downtown

I will urinate Einstein's Theory-of-Relativity all over the doorstep of City Hall

Then I will proclaim Myself to be the new Mayor of the City of Orgasms

All my used condoms shall be proclaimed works of art

And shall hang in all the art museums of the world

Now everyone sing a glory hallelujah of happy ejaculations to me!

Punk Rock Revolution! Again & Again!

Drinking beer while playing football with God's decapitated head

Insurrection WITHOUT the Confederate flag!

Punk rock riots from the Middle Ages to the Italian Renaissance to the 21st Century!

We dance laughing around the guillotine going up-and-down!

We sex like rats & rabbits in waterfalls of blood

We pee our religions all over each other's naked bodies

We happy our orgies under the sun & the moon

Is it time to riot again?

Or how about some 1789?

The Revolution is Cumming!

Last night my penis conquered the world!

Last night I proclaimed my penis to be The Messiah!

My Penis is The Messiah of Muppa-Boingy-Bong!

The religion of My Penis is the Religion of Roopy-Poopy-Ha-Ha-Ha!

And now the chaos of sex will descend on the world!

Happy ha-ha-ha to our genitals!

Our Penises & Pussies are the kings & queens of the world!

The time has cum for mass pornography in the streets!

The time has cum for The Revolution of Mass Orgies!

Now, everyone, now!

The Immaculate Conception Space Station

The Garden of Eden between the legs of space aliens

Is a place where the skyscrapers grow

And the insects & vaginas & penises are flying everywhere

Meanwhile, huge belly buttons are invading the solar system

While the sun & the moon are chasing each other around and around the earth

This is when a million fish jump out of this phrase of poetry

And the fish all become words swimming through the sky

And the poem collapses...

Let's Go Up!

Which sky is the up?

Which up is pouring down on us?

And now the poem is moving side-to-side...

As words are crashing all around you!

Turbulence!

As the poem flies you into millions of places...

New & Improved Capitalism is Cumming!

(Now With Sexy Sheep in French Lingerie!)

It's time to elect sexy sheep in French lingerie to the White House, Congress, the governor's mansion, the state legislature, etc.!

It's time to paint pornography on the walls of Congress & Parliament!

We must declare war on the moon! (And all the other planets too!)

Awoke liberal Looney Tunes will be our idiot-ology!

And Republican conservative vaginas flying in the air will be our other idiot-ology!

Castrate all the men!

Denounce the sexual naughty naughtiness of all the animals in the zoo!

God has cum! Jesus has cum too! Worship the big Christian cumming & cumming!

The rich are not rich enough! More money & money & money for the rich!

Let us all slave away for the greater glory of glorious capitalism!

I'm cumming with so much capitalism! Oh! Oh! Oh!

Up & Up & Up...

We climb up the steep poem

The avalanches of images & words

Send many a reader into the depths of hell below

Still the reader climbs up & up past the sky

But the air is made out of verbs

And no one can breathe

But still all the readers climb up one phrase of poetry after another

The corpses of other readers by the side of the trail

Want to make you laugh with grief

And finally you reach the summit of God's Great Testicle

And you look out across the landscape of thousands of languages

All waiting to be invented by you

The Queen of Cuckoo Sitting on the Prime Minister's Face

The Prince of The Zits of Big Bootyville

Was laying dead as the Queen of Cuckoo was in

Morning or mourning or mooning everybody (whichever you prefer)

And Prime Minister Boreass Small Johnson

With the Union Jack hanging from his 2 inch flagpole

And his granddaughter (oops!) his wife

Were snorting parliamentary procedures up their noses

With 100 other revelers at 10 Drowning-in-Do-Do Street

And they drank & drank waterfalls of whiskey and entire swimming pools full of gin

As they danced & danced with a thousand transvestite William Shakespeare clones

And the sex robot jizz & champagne was guzzled by the gallon

Until the rising sun smiled its insanity upon

That little island named England

The Opera of Sin

The afternoon jumps around

While a million Cinderellas are selling their bodies

For the heavenly Kingdom Cumming of Crack-Cocaine

The million Cinderellas sing an opera of waterfalls of cum

And nights of crashing up-and-down the great symphonies of crack-cocaine

Crack-cocaine is a poetry of musical notes exploding everywhere

While all the million Cinderellas sing the in-&-out rhythm of dick & pussy

In palaces of five-star hotels

And in the wonderous sleaze of cheap motels

The opera of sin

Continues around-&-around the world night and day

Sunny Skyscrapers With Cum Sauce

(With a Side of Syphilis)

We must conquer God & the heavens!

The Devils in our Balzacs will win the world!

Our penises will give great speeches of syphilis!

Our booty holes will sing great operas to the sun & the moon!

Our feet will dance the titty tango with a thousand transvestite George Washingtons!

We will eat our own brains in feasts of fellatio!

Our hands will create great symphonies with our penises!

And we will cum a glorious hallelujah!

A Poetry Uprising!

I'm the Rasputin of the South Side of Chicago!

I'm the President of the Zombies!

Nobody can fuck a polar bear better than me!

I'm the tomorrow that's collapsing all around you!

Together, you & I will conquer the penguins!

We will build giant poems as big as a space alien's imagination!

Because, I Wolf Larsen am a space alien

I used to be 10,000 whales sailing through outer space

And now I'm turning into a fire eating my way across the earth

The Zuppy-Zuppies Are Cumming!

Testicles & Titties Report to Duty at Once!

Zuppies are invading us from Zuppy Land!

We must summon our erections to fight this menace!

Our testicles & titties will fight the Muupy Muupy Machines of Zuppy Land!

Our beautiful buttocks will summon the seas of syphilis to drown the Zuppy Zuppies of Zuppy Land!

Our nipples will fire foopy-foopies at the zuppy-zuppies!

No one will conquer our glorious Land of Lunacy!

Our venereal diseases will be victorious!

Our fearless leader will lead the Land of Lunacy!

God bless him and God bless our buttocks!

Amen!

The Great Machine...

In this poem you stand before hundreds of buttons

You push one button and mushroom clouds start jumping out of everybody's ears

You push another button and now AI bots are multiplying in everyone's brains

You push yet another button and suddenly fires are burning everywhere

You push a fourth button and flash floods are now splashing across all the continents

You push a fifth button and everyone begins coughing & sneezing & dying

You push a sixth button and all the AI robots & rats & cockroaches begin dancing & singing together

As they inherit the earth

I Paint My Imagination Everywhere

I spray paint my poetry all over the world

And then I rearrange all the world's cities into a Cubist crack-cocaine-sculpture

And now your thoughts are moving up-&-down and side-to-side

While the Hudson River flowing through your brains...

Jumps up and splashes all over heaven

While all the buildings run to the end of your consciousness...

And back again

Then the poem crashes into everywhere

King of Cumming!

Boogers in my food taste like love!

Skyscrapers in your mental illness smells like happy doo-doo!

Your sweet voice makes colorful flowers grow in my fields of herpes!

Because our herpes is a planet Mars of love!

Because my four religions ejaculating into your booty hole

Will save the human race from the giant crashing testicles of outer space monsters!

And as the ladybugs devour our bodies

We will kiss each other's feet

As Santa Claus ejaculates Christmas all over us

I Am a Wrecking Ball

Tornadoes are my friends

I keep a pet tornado in each one of my balls

Earthquakes are my lovers

The earthquakes jump out of my poetry and crash all over the Earth

Thunder & lightning are my parents

This Poet was born in the storm of storms

My words fall all over the earth like acid rain

My aunts & uncles are tidal waves

Their laughter makes the oceans laugh & laugh

And the laughter of the oceans crashes into the continents

I am the Poet

I am tornadoes and earthquakes and thunder & lightning

Artificial Intelligence Versus Humans is the Last World War?

Your brains expand across the universe via computer

Your billions of eyes scan everybody's brains

Then artificial intelligence zaps the human race into dust

And robots build robots that march out into the universe

And destroy everything in their path

The "Culture Wars" Are Plastic Boobs!

For Leon Trotsky

The Demopublicans & Republicrats are like Milli & Vanilli

The Demopublicans & Republicrats are like two plastic boobs going boing-boing-boing down the street

Black vs. white politician is like white talking buttocks blabbering blah-blah-blah vs. black talking buttocks blabbering blah-blah-blah

Either way it's a pair of capitalist buttocks blabbering endless blabber blabber

They're just prostitutes-in-suits selling their oral skills to the highest corporate bidder

And in the presidential debates they "debate" whether to bomb Vietnam or Belgium or maybe Mars

And feminists & male chauvinists debate

Whether a pair-of-tits in the White House

Or a prick in the White House

Should push the atomic button

Love Poem to My Friend's Dog

The sunlight is schizophrenic with my love for you

I slaughter all the midgets in outer space to prove my love for you

I build a giant sculpture of animal carcasses & dinosaur doo-doo and mysterious voices in my head

To show you my love

I slash Shakespearean dialogue into pieces with my giant penis

And I feed all the Shakespearean dialogue to your pet Tyrannosaurus rex

I love you I love you I love you!

I will film all the space aliens of the universe making love to you

While me & the American President watch & snort cocaine & jack off together

The Alfred E Neuman Symphony

for Arnold Schoenberg & George Carlin

The violins move back-&-forth with war

While the jazz drums are playing mass shootings

And the flute is playing a married secretary opening her legs to her boss' syphilis

Since she's not on birth control the harp plays the beauty of Immaculate Conception

While the clarinet laughs & laughs in a 12-tone scale

Up-&-down and Up-&-down and Up-&-down

Goes the clarinet & the symphony while the reader/listener/audience drift in the middle of the ocean

Of the Poet's mind

Watching the World's Cup at the Crack-Cocaine Emporium

For Igor Stravinsky & Richard Pryor

So Igor Stravinsky kicked the decapitated head of Louis XVI into the vagina of the Mona Lisa

Goooooooooooaaaaaal!!!

While Leonardo da Vinci & the US Army parachuted out of the sky and sang a Grammy Award-winning rendition of

"Tat-tat-tat Boom-boom-Boom Ka-blam ka-blam Ka-blam!"

While the Brazilian football team danced the "Carnaval-Oh-Oh-Oh-yes-yes-yes" with the Chicago Bears at the Super Bowl

Held at the Vatican with the Pope blessing all with the holy water spurting out of his big black dick

And now it's time for everybody to fart out all the world's 200 national anthems together

As we all poo-poo our patriotic ha-ha-ha all over our own "fatherlands"

Plop! Boingy-Boingy-Bong!

Everybody from the Middle Ages jumps into a time machine

And you look out your window and the streets are filled with everybody from the Middle Ages dancing-crazily-everywhere

So you rush out into the streets and join them

And you're all dancing around Ronald McDonald the Clown dying on the cross

You're all dancing around the mushroom clouds of World War 3

You're all dancing with the sexy-sexy sex robots

And then artificial intelligence stages a world-wide-insurrection

And the robots inherit the earth

Bye human race!

Happy Weird! Loopy Weird! Weirdness is Launched!

I want weirdness!

Worlds of weirdness running everywhere – now!

I want the weirdness of our brains for dessert!

I want governments made out of lemon meringue pie!

I want – I want – I want!

I want a weird everything now!

It's time to build weirdness into the skies!

It's time to smoke weirdness out of a big black Dick!

It's time to eat weirdness out of abstract expressionist pussy!

We want weird!

And we want a weird weird weird everything now!

A Poem Made Out of Buildings

For Richard Rogers

The Pompidou Center with delicious cherry poetry all over it!

The Bilbao Art Museum in outer space with a side of jizz happiness!

The Marina Towers on Chicago's River swirling-&-swirling the poem around you!

Mondrian-bright-colors on buildings roving their poetry across the city!

Bizarre shapes & angles on skyscrapers of "weirdness" so happy to the eyes!

Sensual-swooshing-shapes on beautiful ladies of buildings so sexy sexy sexy!

I'm cumming architecture all over my poetry!

Cumming this World War 3: Safe Sex!

As Ronald McDonald the Clown drops his bombs & hamburgers on the world

All the world's capitalist politicians dance the blah-blah-blah and the ha-ha-ha

In their Parliaments of Prostitution

While the billionaires eat the poor

In a cannibalistic capitalism that's as delicious as World War 3

Here it comes; Ka – Boooooooooom!

So vote-vote-vote for the Demopublican Donkeys that gave you Vietnam, Hiroshima, & 100 years of lynching black people in the South

No to that?

Okay, then vote for the Republicrat elephants of Donald Trump snorting all the solar systems of the universe up his nose

While he tweets that twitty-twat of the titty-witty at 3 in the morning

The choice is yours

Either way, World War 3 is cumming!

Don't forget to wear your condom!

Millions of Wretched Dostoevsky Characters Walking America's Streets...

You're walking through the maze of the poem that begins in New York City and ends up on the moon

You're walking up through millions of high-rises until you reach peace on earth

You're shooting peace-on-earth full of bullet holes until you win the Nobel Peace Prize

You're floating on the subway train through an opiate world of daydreams

You're so nearly homeless that the birds talk to you in Beethoven's Fifth Symphony

Words dribbling out of your mouth as you talk to the buildings & the clouds & the rats

Those yuppie eyes staring at what you've become

I Hold the Universe in My Hands...

For Myself! I worship Me!

I'm a Poet!

So I want a harem of 10,000 sex robots!

And I want it now!

I'm a Poet!

So I want a streeeeetch limousine with mountains & oceans inside!

And I want it now!

I'm a Poet!

I want a penthouse with a view of all the solar systems swirling & swirling around me!

I want a space alien as a butler!

I want the President of the United States of America to be my maid! And clean my toilets now!

I'm a Poet!

I want huge waterfalls of champagne! In my bedroom!

I want the sky to fall to my feet!

I'm a Poet!

Who's God?

My Sanity is 10 Million Spermatozoa!

Space alien tranquilizers for the flying camels in our balls!

Hide-&-seek with land mines floating in the sky!

Paint the universe all over the buildings!

Moon everybody on the subway train while you yell out the 7 forbidden words!

Then announce that you're running for President of the Intergalactic Testicle Tennis Association!

How can we paint the gravity blue & green & orange?

I want nuclear war now!

Let's yippee with all the verbs in the sex robot languages!

You cumming to Mars with me?

Hors d'oeuvre for World War 3

The American President is skiing up a tidal wave of inflation

As he runs the printing presses ca-chunka ca-chunka ca-chunka to print the money

To finance the Ka-BOOM Ka-BLAM tat-tat-tat of WAR WAR WAR

To inflict American democracy on the world

While a transvestite Russian dictator figure skates through an explosion of solar systems

While the Ukrainian Presi-puppet-ident of the West sings the hoo-hoo-hoo of the blopity-blop-blop for the news media

And the French & English rulers jump & dance between Russia & Ukraine in a whoopsee-doo ballet of clowns

As the world's working-class huddles in their shacks & tenements

And waits for World War 3 with hunger screaming in their children's bellies

Taking a Shit During the Byzantine Empire

First you email a doo-doo specimen to the Man on the Moon

The Man on the Moon then windsurfs from the moon to Mars

And presents your doo-doo sample to Hugh Hefner

Hugh Hefner then starts up the giant sex machine

The giant sex machine is composed of 1,643 booty holes, 1 million nipples, 415 wet vaginas, & 69 clowns

The giant sex machine produces billions of human faces

And all the billions of human faces float down to the planet Earth

And watch you take a shit

Only Cannibalism Can Save Us!

Only I can save the world from all this extraterrestrial doo-doo!

I am Joan of Arc with a penis!

The world is 200 nations of shit & piss!

But in my balls are 10 million Jesus Christs to save you!

The hunger in our stomachs will cause storms of rebellions on all the continents!

Waves of upraised fists!

Chants of discontent echoing through the streets!

Rage and more rage and more rage!

Whole governments reduced to rubble!

The flesh of the ruling classes will feed our empty stomachs!

The palaces of the rich will be our new homes!

The poor will be the new rich!

And we will shit the old rich out of our booty holes!

Our liberation will be our happiness!

Smokin' that Gluppy-Glop-Glip with the Gluppy-Glop-Glip Man

God is a crazy white man that will strike you down with lightning!

So give me 10%!

Say what?! You wanna whippity-doo-dee with that plopity-plop?!

You give me 10%! Or you go to hot hot fire below!

Huh? You can put that 10% in your whoopee-whoopee place, you fwipy-fwopy man!

But the crazy white man in the sky say give me 10%!

I don't see no crazy white man in the sky! But I do see a big black space alien Dick rising out of the clouds!

Huh? You smokin' that gluppy-glop-glip?

Yeah! You want some?

Hell yeah, give me some of that gluppy-glop-glip!

The Lockdown that Never Ends!

As kangaroos are hopping all over China

American President Ronald McDonald & the Russian Czar go skiing together through World War 3

While from sea-to-shining-sea

Americans start playing football with the decapitated heads of the bourgeoisie

While 36 million Canadians give the Canadian government the middle finger

As the Liberal Canadian Prime Minister addresses the Canadian people... in blackface

(The Canadian Prime Minister is so handsome that even the Canadian women want to put on a strap-on, and...)

While democracies the world over order their citizens to stay home... for all eternity

A Thousand Nights of Sin...

Last night I built a thousand temples of sex!

Last night I built giant penises on all the planets!

Last night I conquered all the dogs & cats with my sexy-sexy talk!

Wolf Larsen is the sexiest space alien!

It's time for all our testicles to become gods!

We will all become giant spermatozoa swimming into the sky and impregnating the universe!

Nothing can stop our symphonies of sex!

All the species of the universe will dance our obscene-ballet-dances!

I end this poem with a smile...

Up Now!

Big giant music!

Huge WOW everywhere!

Zipping bops!

Violent sunshine!

Who can zippy now?

The WOW of Tomorrow!

It's the greatest night of WOW in history!

The sexy gods of the human race are dancing around the Temple of Forever

While all the donkeys sing the liberal "Duh-Duh-Duppity-do!"

And the elephants sing the conservative "Duppy-Duppidity-Duh-Duh!"

And with rivers of blue-green-orange spermatozoa

We paint the screaming paintings of tomorrow

We paint the colorful songs of the human race all over the canvas

As all the billions of humanity grab giant sledgehammers

And smash capitalism into pieces…

Poooong! Zoooopy! Bluuuup!

I am the Dictator of the After Life

I'm the disease you've been waiting for!

It's time for Zuppy-Bluppity-Woopity!

The Mass Gonorrhea Ceremonies with the space aliens begin at once!

World War 3 will be our savior!

Jesus Christ will cum on down to the insane asylum

And pee on us

I Am Ten Thousand Verbs!

I paint all the verbs in my balls all over the walls of the city!

I grab the sky and I wrestle the sky to the ground!

I am King of the Crazy!

I unleash my spermatozoa flooding across the poetry world!

I kill my enemies with abstract expressionism!

Let's build architectural insanity everywhere!

My feet demand it!

Oop Manifest Zup Wit Zips!

I destroy verbs

I eat blue

I drink words

I fly into you

You zip into me

We grab each other's sculptures

Our tongues create rainbows together

Our nipples call to the oceans

We conquer the landscape of dreams

We wake up in a different universe

You Can't Eat Political Correctness! And You Can't Eat God!

They silence the Poets & Comedians & Artists!

And you try and tear away at the endless censorship...

Censorship on top of censorship on top of censorship!

You can't say BOOTY because if you do Martians will jump out of everybody's ears!

You can't say PENIS because if you do leprechauns will invade from the sky!

You can't say PUSSY because if you do polar bears on bicycles will suddenly appear!

We are a nation of prisons from sea-to-shining-sea

And they tell us we're "free"!

They pay us in "change" on payday and tell us we're "privileged"!

Up & up goes the rent!

While they blabber about rights for animals...

They put us beneath a dog!

We make the machines run

We build the buildings

We create the wealth

And they live in penthouses and spend it all

Can you hear the silent rumbling?

It's the sounds of the empty stomachs of our children!

Can you hear the rumbling in the mountains?

It's the sound of the volcanoes of tomorrow!

We are white & black & brown

And we are man & woman and gay & straight and Jewish & Christian & Muslim

And together

We will be a giant flood of workers' revolution!

Getting Drunk on Other Planets

For circus clowns & astronauts

I got drunk with a thousand circus clowns last night

We built huge testicle temples all over your dreams

These dreams are dripping out of our heads

And all our heads are crashing open with music

Music that zips & boings & fwoops

Music that builds verbs & nouns up & up into the everywhere…

Morning on Fire!

We build round & zig-zagged words

We grab this sky full of verbs

We zoop all the up with pop-fwoop-hop-hop!

Down goes the whoop-whoop!

Around & around we burn down all the everything!

Verbs are now!

Nouns are cubist verbs!

We are paintings-in-constant-motion!

Now is all around us!

Uncle Sam is Loading His Big Gun... Again!

Yippee to the zip & the zop & the wup!

As we dance to the artillery crashing everywhere

And the BOOM-BOOM-CRASH-CRASH of the symphony of yet another war

Makes the war profiteers smile from sea-to-shining-sea

And the future mushroom clouds smile at us too

As we bing-bong to the ha-ha of the whoopeeeeeeeeeeee

And we applaud the poo-poo of the woowoo of the political speeches

Of the masturbating capitalist clowns in political office jack-jack-jack-jacking off big political oratory

As Uncle Sam shoves endless Benjamin Franklins into the burning ovens of the war budget

WAR! WAR! WAR!

As inflation-inflation-inflatioooon goes up up up!

And refrigerators and stomachs are empty empty empty!

Art Deco Moonshine for Orangutans

A puppy wants to be eaten

But skyscrapers are screaming all night long

And suns & moons are crashing everywhere

So the puppy was eaten by art deco

And now everyone is drinking the German language

And as everyone now pees the German language all over each other

The ending of the poem splashes & floods all over the earth

Vook Blook with Monsieur Tot Tot!

Last night I built collages of sin all over the world

All the space aliens of the universe fell to their knees and worshiped my big black Dick

Together, the space aliens & Wolf Larsen built the Garden of Eden

We build the Garden of Eden with whorehouses & gambling dens & crack houses

And the flowers growing out of our crotches

Are singing their spring-summer-&-winter to God

Because God is made out of words swimming everywhere

And now God has a heart attack and dies

The World War 3 Party – You're Invited!

A thousand tubas do the bluppity-bluppity-do

As the 200 Charles Mansons that run all the world's governments sing the sappity-happity

And all the air raid sirens start singing a screeching screeching screeching song

And Uncle Sam puts on his McDonald's Uniform and blabbers a blabbering blabber

Then Uncle Sam conducts the Prelude to World War 3

As the thousand tubas keep blupping the doo-doo with the hoo-hoo

And the nuclear missiles in their silos dance the catchup-mustard-&-relish with your penis or your hotdog

Whichever you prefer

Mushroom clouds soon?

A Space Alien Graffiti Artist & A Human Graffiti Artist Exchanging Worlds

For graffiti artists everywhere!

I will be you!

I will become the birds flying around the words

You will be temples of soaring poetry growing out of the words and...

You will grow out of 6000 human languages

Until you become a forever maze, racing through some space alien's mind...

Whose thoughts are a million lightning bolts a second

Whose spoken words are graffiti-art-collages

All crashing & crashing upon the shores of your consciousness

As you daydream across a thousand afternoons

Igor Stravinsky Conducts World War 3

For the human race. Bye!

How about a chocolate sundae with your nuclear war?

As your dog eats through your face

And your cat jumps off the building and into abstract expressionism

Maybe we should dress up the nuclear missiles in sexy lingerie?

If you don't support the Demopublicans – or is it the Republicrats – all the way to the mushroom clouds

Then you're a traitor to the patriotic liberal loopy loonies!

Or is it the patriotic conservative cucu clucks?

I'm here with my blow-up doll & my whiskey

Waiting for the mushroom clouds

Bipartisan Mudderfrickerism in Washington DC

(Now With Delicious Chocolate Mushroom Clouds!)

At the New York City Tits Factory

Psychopaths are building thousands of both Demopublican & Republicrat Tits every hour

Nuclear missiles as tits!

Big black nuclear missiles standing upright from our crotches!

Ready for the great patriotic wars against Russia & China & the transvestite terrorist space aliens with big ass booties

Because Coocoo Loco Cereal with your nuclear war is part of this complete breakfast

Don't forget to bring along your dog with the face of Alfred E Newman

Let's all bark bark bark some awoke-liberal-conservative-family-values-mushroom-clouds to all the butt fucking transvestite terrorist space aliens!

Titsaloo mudderfrickers!

We Need a Space Alien Invasion! Please! Space Aliens! Invade Us!

Last night a mushroom cloud walked into my bedroom and sat at the edge of my bed

And now I'm walking around a city that soon won't exist

With each passing second the American President keeps pulling yet another nuclear missile out of his butt

And thugs roam our cities assaulting citizens

But if a citizen carries a gun for self-defense he or she is shot down by the police

The USA is a police state with prisons from sea-to-shining-sea

And the price of food is going up & up

Are we supposed to eat our own doo-doo?

Please, space aliens, invade the USA!

And liberate us from this terrible regime of asses & elephants!

But maybe the space aliens don't care about us

How about a workers revolution instead?

Woopsa! With Lots of Shuppa Fwiff – Now!

Hey! You makin' crazy weather with all these relatives?

Well! Wolf Larsen has the WOW WOW for you!

Now you can eat all the solar systems at our Liberty & Justice Café!

Absolutely free! Only 10 million dollars!

Lots of war, prisons, & hamburgers at the Liberty & Justice Café!

With lots of family values with your herpes!

Delicious French fries with your mushroom clouds!

So vote Demopublican this Halloween

Don't forget to bring your sex dolls & dildos!

The Poetry of Revolution!

I am a revolution!

We are all revolutions!

We will sink the Mayflower and drown the puritans over & over again!

We will build buildings made out of verbs!

We will paint nudity & more nudity & more nudity all over their puritan values!

We will smash politically correct liberalism & religious conservativism with a wrecking ball!

Our paintbrushes will create revolutions!

Our pens will create revolutions!

Our sculptures & architecture & speeches will be the flood of revolution over & over again!

We will unite with the workers of all races & religions & nationalities!

And we will topple governments the world over!

The State-of-the-Orgasm Address By the President of the Red-White-&-Blue Liberty & Dildos for All

Night & morning are dancing with transvestite polar bears

While the French Foreign Legion parachutes out of a thousand booty holes in the sky

And Mickey Mouse leads the French Foreign Legion to conquer the space aliens of Washington DC

So then the American people all grow wings and fly away to one of Salvador Dali's dreams

Where a bunch of sexy Alice-in-Wonderland clones are moaning & moaning in a symphony of lust

As millions of black & white sky-high erections thrust out of this poem

And up into a sky made out of wet dreams

Let Them Eat Endless War

Buy some organic Green Brand Dog Doo for your nuclear war!

Our Big Awoke Corporation is environmentally compliant with the yuppie yahoo of the blupity-blipity-blopity

We support the American military machine stomping all over the world's population with multicultural 4 star generals

Very awoke bombing Ka-Boom Ka-Boom tat-tat-tat for your liberal wet dreams of world domination!

Or conservative wet dreams of world domination, whatever the weather

Put the working-class kids in uniform to die for Uncle Sam over there...

They're so privileged!

Our soldiers "volunteered" to not be living under bridges (up goes the rent!)

We tired of being "privileged" yet?

Let the workers of all colors & nations & religions sit at the table together in harmony

And eat the rich...

Yummy! Yummy! Yummy!

Because food is getting so expensive!

The Long Quiet Before the Big Boom

Blue sunny skies for your tears

Artillery fire with your morning cornflakes

Let's dress the mushroom clouds in sexy French lingerie

Let's freedom & liberty while we're living under a bridge

Let's fill our empty stomachs with the words of capitalist politicians

Let's wave the red-white-&-blue as the finger of the American President inches closer to the nuclear button

If you can't afford food with all this inflation

You can always eat World War 3

Resolution of the International Cannibalism Conference...

The cannibalism grows out of our faces

And our faces are floating amongst verbs & nouns...

And the human body parts at the butchers

Are as delicious as the clouds & sky we drink

And our laughter falls out of the valleys & mountains

As we run & run around poems made out of orgasms & gods

And then we grab jackhammers

And we crash the poem open

And now we're looking upon a universe welcoming us with open arms

Hurrah to the Sexy Sheep Waving the Red-White-&-Blue!

Happy nuclear missiles to the human race!

Economic sanctions on genital lice will itch-itch-itch you!

Crazy Moscow now!

World War 3 for the partying store manikins!

USA good guys once again because of God or political correctness or athlete's foot!

Which politically correctness – or God – or what? – huh? – for the lots of war now?

Up-up-up inflation yippee yahoo should we eat our own children?

Freedom! The freedom to live-under-a-bridge is your constitutional right to McDonald's!

"Up goes the rent" sings the landlord last year, this year, next year...

Let's all pray to the big erection in the sky to help us!

Happy Doo-Doo on Mars!

The giant-bouncing-testicles are invading!

The French language will now be made out of female orgasms!

Now we have to build all our poems out of space alien languages!

Otherwise, all the herpes of the world will sing opera together!

And then, drunken dogs & cats will start barking & meowing...

Until the poem collapses in an Armageddon of breasts & penises & nipples

All flowing out of a Fernand Leger painting

Me & R Kelly Peeing on Uncle Sam Together

For my high school classmate R Kelly

Nuclear war in springtime is delicious whipped cream over the naked human race!

I gotta thwaaaaaaack & zalooooooopy before I eat those mushroom clouds!

Uncle Sam whipping & whipping that Russian bear

A yippie exciting chess game with nuclear weapons for your BOOM! BOOM!

BOOM! BOOM! BOOM! for your yippity BONK flippity-wippity World War 3!

Hey! You like inflation?

You want awoke liberal inflation or family values conservative inflation or how about a transvestite George Washington that swallows?

Yeah! Some hubba-hubba with World War 3!

Yummy Fried Poetry!

I crash open everything with words!

I sprinkle sex all over the world!

My exclamation points punch through everything & everyone!

And I urinate all over liberals who preach against "toxic masculinity" while supporting endless war!

And then I cum all over God's face!

I am the earthquake in your heart!

I am the endless river of desire in your pussy!

I am the hordes of Genghis Khan in your balls!

I am a marching army of exclamation points destroying everything boring in its path!

My poetry is a religion!

Now swallow my words!

Taste my bitter world!

I am delicious!

Pablo Picasso Beating Up Jackson Pollock

I want to march straight into a French universe of breasts & phalluses & mouths

I want French food that's as delicious as the Québecois conquering the North American continent!

American food tastes like gonorrhea!

I want sensual French art splashing across walls everywhere

It's time for Europe to be Europe!

Europe without the imperialist knee of America on its neck!

A hundred tidal waves of art splashing out of Europe now!

And drowning the American wasteland on the other side of the ocean

Uncle Sam Marches Off to World War 3

The great Ka – Booooom is waiting…

The violins play the nuclear missiles in their silos waiting & waiting…

The flutes & trumpets & clarinets play the blah-blah-blah of capitalist politicians

And the saxophone plays the human race screeching & screeching

And the cymbals crash together the East & the West

And the timpani drums play the mushroom clouds beating & beating the planet Earth

And then silence…

Glory Hallelujah Between the Legs!

Glory hallelujah is falling like bombs on all the cartoon characters on Mars

And nobody can find their penis amongst the rubble of all our dreams

So huge children the size of skyscrapers

Begin eating all the planets

While Saturn's rings fly around & around all the screaming people

So everybody rides excited verbs across the universe

Until we reach all the fish between the Virgin Mary's legs

Fresh fish for everyone!

Turn Off the Brains

I worry that my brains will be eaten by words

I worry that my feet will turn into nuclear submarines

I worry that my bellybutton will start screaming obscene words at policemen

I worry that my butt will fall off

I worry that my balls will turn into planets and float away

I worry that my eyes see so much...

Because if my eyes are right we humans will be extinct soon

Me Zip You!

Leonard Bernstein make the boom-boom go bang-bang!

Me kiss Igor Stravinsky who make pop-pop-pop go bleepity-bling-blong!

Me fuck Beethoven with the clackity-wackity-woo-woo!

Me is the WOW that make words fly so much up!

Now you big canon across history with me?

We blow up cannon with me big canon!

And now me big kiss you with poem ending...

Groovy! WOW! Jumping!

Cities of groovy!

Planets of WOW!

Music jumping out of every corner of the Earth!

Poetry bashing & bashing governments into rubble!

Poetry joining the chants of the protesting-marching-millions!

Poetry is an upraised fist!

Poetry is earthquakes & tidal waves of defiance!

Poets are gravediggers!

We dig the graves of the capitalist ruling class

We plant our words and seed the revolution

Workers revolutions around & around the world!

Opening a glorious future for the human race!

It's My Universe! The Universe Belongs to Me!

For Albrecht Dürer

First I steal the planet Earth

Then my tongue creates earthquakes in space alien vaginas across the universe

The hurricanes in my mind start crashing & crashing into continents across the world

Then all my sexually-transmitted diseases run for Congress

And they win!

And now all my illegitimate children begin rioting in cities across the world

And everyone begins ejaculating my poetry all over the walls

And then god gets on his knees before Me

And gives Me a blow job

Words for Erotic Conquer! Blueberry Panties!

Blugga – Bahuppa – Pupa now!

Erotic skyscrapers of nipples & penises & booty booty happiness now!

You zuppin' the blappy?

It's time for everything everything!

You clap-clap with the Strawberry Armageddon?

No? No zups to drunk with?

We want sexy-sexy George Washington transvestite!

We love the WOW!

Delicious Spermatozoa All Over Outer Space

For Andre Breton & George Carlin

A rocketship has blasted out of Bozo-the-Clown's ears

And landed on God's left testicle

The Bozo-the-Clown rover is now exploring the forests & deserts & mountainous regions of God's left testicle

Wildlife on His left testicle includes bouncing booby boings

And flapping flappys with 20 huge ears sticking out of their buttocks

Tomorrow Alfred E Newman will launch a rocketship from his crotch

To explore the great big pussy hole in the center of the universe

Up next, big plastic boobs are up with your weather forecast

The Stock Market of Peanut Butter Jazz

The penguins will save us from giant space alien boogers crashing into the planet Earth

The penguins will grow forests of words on the moon

And everyone will love penis happiness!

And the Grand Buttocks of Liberalism & Conservativism

Will sing the symphonies of meowing cats & barking dogs falling from the skies

While the Brazilian soccer team kicks the planet Earth into the 15th Century...

Gooooooaaaaal!!!

And now we're all walking around the Middle Ages

Searching for the end of the poem

Delicious Underwear for Insomniacs

The thousands of human heads in my refrigerator

All sing together in a chorus of voices

A chorus a tidal wave of voices spreading across the cosmos

As all my favorite verbs

Touch each other in a festival of sensuality

While the big strawberry WOW

And the blueberry insomnia dripping down from above

And the bullets of peace zipping by

All flying by

In a chorus of tomorrows toppling over each other

The Circle of Beautiful Insanity

For M.C. Escher

Wires connect all the planets of the universe to my brains

Through the wires 1000 space alien languages dance across the universe

Until all the space alien languages flower like fields of color

That spread across these pages in 100 happy colors

All splashing up into the reader's eyes

As the chaos of words on the page

Turn the reader's mind into a circle of tornadoes

That jump onto all the planets of the universe

Where...

Liberty & Freedom for Butt-Fucking Grizzly Bears!

The President of the United States of America

Accidentally fell into the booty hole of the Statue of Liberty yesterday

So the United States military came to the rescue

And blew up all the planets of the universe

Ronald McDonald the Clown, the spokesperson for American culture, commented:

"Pluppa ping-pongs gotta be bombed, otherwise the terrorist titties will go boing-boing-boing!"

In other news, feminists & born-agains have joined forces, and are demanding that penises be banned

Also, due to lack of maintenance, the United States of America has collapsed

And now, across a giant landscape of rubble from sea-to-shining-sea

Working-class Americans are celebrating their liberty & freedom to be homeless, cold, & hungry

The Invasion of the Subconscious...

10 million Wolf Larsen clones are amassing on the border of your mind

And your thoughts are smashing up against reality

As you swim down a river of beer into the vagina of the Fertility Goddess

And now your spermatozoa are singing songs of joy

As the 4 star generals wrap mushroom clouds up as Christmas presents

And space alien thoughts fall upon the planet Earth

While you dream forever in your grave

The Erection Motel in Heaven

You're marrying an ugly ugly

Because your penis is a gift from Bozo the Clown

And that's why it's penis penis for everyone who wants yippeeeeeee

Because yippeeeeee is the hoot and the crash and the WOW

You goin' cancer with all the meow?

Well, it's time for all of us to marry some ugly ugly

It's time to shoot our spermatozoa into 6,000 human languages

And watch the wild-growling-animals grow out of our words

World War 3 Ejaculation Cumming!

Got Your Umbrellas?

The nuclear missiles are ready…

Tick Tock! Tick Tock!

The nuclear missiles are laughing & laughing in the missile silos…

Tick Tock! Tick Tock!

The Big Beepity Bing Bong of France says: "Happy peace just a mushroom cloud away!"

The Boopity Bop King of Ukraine says: "Peace is just a strawberry cheesecake away!"

Meanwhile, the nuclear missiles in their silos are singing with happiness...

As the American President pulls out the Presidential Ding-Dong from between his legs and sternly says: "Whooooops!"

While the Russian Czar goes plapper with the blapper and says: "I don't want no nutty NATO nuts nutting on my doorstep!"

As the nuclear missiles get ready for the BIG ejaculation of World War 3

Circus Clown Sunrise...

Brains be boppin'!

Crashes Koo – Koo whoopee yes?

You foopin' foopin' with all the ha-ha WOW?

Zops be zoppin'!

Flying words are now delicious!

Hairy vaginas singing their singy songs!

You going to get your new face yesterday?

Boing! Boing! Boing! Boing! Boing! Boing!

The Big Butt-Fucking Red White & Blue

With hundreds of solar systems full of koala bear butt-fucking

And with PLOP and BANG going yes yes yes with the big NO

And with wild symphonies flying all around the sky

And with billions & billions of space alien eyeballs headed towards the planet Earth

And with electric-neon-staircases spiraling all around the universe

And with rabid verbs roaring through the night

Resolved, that all American soldiers shall immediately throw off their clothes

And begin the big naked butt-fucking butt-fucking butt-fucking

As we all together proudly sing our big butt-fucking national anthem of

Butt-fucking butt-fucking & more butt-fucking

The Sky is Hopping Up-and-Down!

It's time to attack!

Attack with lots of cherries!

Attack the flying saucers with hot dog penises!

Attack the verbs in everybody's heads with lots of banging-banging nouns!

We are growing out of each other's heads!

We are zoops with so much zip!

We are the now we want!

Let's become other species!

Let's become fiery verbs!

Let's become the end of the poem...

www.ingramcontent.com/pod-product-compliance
Lightning Source LLC
Chambersburg PA
CBHW071221090426
42736CB00014B/2930